Original title:

Reflections of the Celestial Soul

Author: Sebastian Sarapuu

ISBN HARDBACK: 978-1-80561-292-6

ISBN PAPERBACK: 978-1-80561-853-9

Explorations of the Glimmering Void

In the depths where silence sleeps,
Stars like whispers start to creep.
Galaxies twirl in cosmic dance,
Lost in dreams of distant chance.

A shimmer here, a flicker there,
Ancient tales hang in the air.
Time drifts slow, like misty dew,
In this realm of shades and hue.

Nebulas paint the night with grace,
A canvas vast, an endless space.
Curiosity ignites a spark,
Exploring realms both bright and dark.

Voids that call with silent roar,
Secrets hidden, forevermore.
Each heartbeat echoes, soft, profound,
As wonders in the dark abound.

With every glance, a puzzle spun,
The glimmering void, yet to be won.
In this expanse, we chase the light,
Finding solace in the night.

So here I stand, a wanderer bold,
In infinite dreams, stories unfold.
The glimmering void, a siren's song,
Calling me to where I belong.

Dreams Woven in Stardust

In the night where silence breathes,
Whispers of hope on gentle leaves.
Stars above, a guiding light,
Weaving dreams in velvet night.

Each wish cast through twinkling skies,
A dance of fate where magic lies.
Hearts entwined, spirits soar,
In the cosmos, we seek more.

Galaxies swirl in our embrace,
Finding warmth in the vast space.
Fingers trace the paths unseen,
In stardust, we are serene.

With every spark, new tales arise,
A symphony of lullabies.
Together we'll chase eternity,
In dreams woven, wild and free.

A tapestry of time and grace,
Bringing us close in this sacred place.
As dawn breaks the spell we've spun,
Our journey together has just begun.

Light Traces on a Dark Canvas

On blackened skies, colors ignite,
Brush strokes of dreams, pure delight.
Whispers of hope paint the night,
Bringing forth the dawn's first light.

Each twinkle, a secret shared,
In the unknown, we are bared.
Life's canvas, so vast, profound,
In shadows of night, beauty is found.

Mirrored stars in deep reflection,
Guide our hearts in pure connection.
With every hue, stories unfold,
A masterpiece crafted, bold.

Colors fade but memories stay,
In light's embrace, we find our way.
A dance of shades, dark and bright,
Crafting peace in endless night.

From darkness, our spirits arise,
In the glow, we realize.
Life's palette is rich and grand,
Each stroke tells of hope at hand.

Breath of Interstellar Serenity

In the void where silence dwells,
Echoes of peace, soft as bells.
Stars breathe life in cosmic dreams,
Unraveling fate in gentle streams.

Celestial winds whisper low,
Bringing calm with every flow.
In the stillness, hearts align,
Finding solace in the divine.

Gravity's pull, tender and light,
Guides us through the endless night.
Floating on the breath of time,
In blissful state, we start to climb.

Moments linger, eternity calls,
Through the cosmos, love enthralls.
On wings of stardust, we drift free,
In interstellar serenity.

With every heartbeat, the stars hum,
Tales of where we've yet to come.
Together we soar, hand in hand,
In this tranquil, timeless land.

The Song of Wandering Stars

In the sea of night, they roam,
Each star a story, far from home.
Melodies weave in cosmic grace,
Songs of longing in endless space.

They twinkle bright, they fade away,
Echoing hopes of yesterday.
In the void, they twirl and spin,
A symphony that draws us in.

With every flash, a tale is spun,
Life's great dance has just begun.
Over horizons, they will glide,
Through the cosmos, side by side.

Together, they shine, a fleeting dance,
In the darkness, seize your chance.
Guided by light, we travel far,
Chasing dreams among the stars.

Each wandering note, a tale of grace,
Sings of love in this vast space.
In the silence, hear their call,
The song of stars unites us all.

Between the Moons of Memory

In whispers soft the shadows play,
Through time's embrace they drift away.
The moons of memory softly glow,
Illuminating paths we know.

Each secret held in quiet sighs,
Beneath the watch of starry skies.
Echoes dance in twilight's light,
Carving dreams in silent night.

A tapestry of moments spun,
In fading light, though we have won.
The stories linger, never fade,
In hearts, the memories are laid.

With every breath, the past we weave,
In gentle folds, our hearts believe.
Between the moons, we find our place,
In timeless love, an endless grace.

Harmonics of the Celestial Body

A symphony in silence shares,
The echoes of the cosmic layers.
Notes that twirl in starlit flight,
Compose a song in cosmic night.

The planets hum, a rhythmic flow,
In harmony, they gently glow.
Galaxies spin their vibrant thread,
In unity, the universe is spread.

Through cosmic winds, the tides will shift,
As melodies begin to lift.
With every heartbeat, stars arise,
Creating art in velvet skies.

In shadows deep, the sounds unite,
A cosmic dance that feels just right.
Harmonics weave a dreamer's lore,
In every note, we seek for more.

Skies Adorned in Silver Dust

The dusk unveils the night's embrace,
With silver dust in velvet space.
Each star a jewel, brightly shined,
In endless awe, we seek, we find.

The whispers glide on evening's breath,
In twilight's glow, we lose our depth.
Soft beams of light, they gently play,
Creating art in night's ballet.

A canvas painted by the night,
With constellations holding tight.
Dreams take flight on wings of hope,
In silver trails, we learn to cope.

With starlit paths beneath our feet,
The universe feels so complete.
Adorned in wonders, skies will trust,
Our hearts alight in silver dust.

Awakening the Celestial Dream

A dawn of wonders calls to me,
In whispers of the galaxy.
The stars conspire in silent schemes,
Awakening our deepest dreams.

In twilight's grace, the night unfolds,
With tales of love, both new and old.
The cosmos breathes in vibrant hues,
Each heartbeat sings the ancient blues.

From shadows dark, the light will rise,
Illuminating secret skies.
With every pulse, the mystic's art,
Awakens softly in the heart.

The universe reveals its face,
In the dance of time and space.
In dreams, we merge, we spin, we gleam,
Awakening the celestial dream.

Dance of the Luminous Spirits

In the night, whispers twirl,
Luminous beings gently swirl.
A ballet on the cosmic floor,
Echoing light, forevermore.

Twilight's grace in every sway,
Stars ignite in a celestial play.
Hearts align with the astral song,
In this dance, we all belong.

Flickering flames, a shared embrace,
Galactic rhythms, time and space.
With every step, a silence breaks,
Awakening dreams that the night makes.

Voices of starlight softly weave,
In their glow, we dare believe.
Spirits twine in radiant glee,
Together, we create the sea.

A dance etched in the void's vast art,
Painting the cosmos, heart to heart.
With every turn, new souls ignite,
In this luminous dance tonight.

Starlit Mosaic of the Soul

Scattered sparks on midnight's loom,
Crafting tales that linger, loom.
Each star a piece of dreams ajar,
Forming the map of who we are.

Colors dance in the cosmic tide,
Emotions shining, nothing to hide.
In the stillness, spirits play,
A mosaic bright, come what may.

Fragments rich, in silence sing,
Harmonies of the heart take wing.
Each moment a brush, each breath a hue,
Painting the essence of me and you.

In the depths where shadows lie,
Light awakens, never shy.
Every shimmer holds a story told,
A starlit tapestry, brave and bold.

The universe spins, a vibrant swirl,
Each heartbeat a pearl in the whirl.
In this mosaic, paths intertwine,
A dance of souls, your light and mine.

Evoking the Galaxies Within

Deep in silence, the echoes swell,
Galaxies whisper, secrets they tell.
Inward journeys, vast and bold,
Universes waiting to be told.

Stars ignite in the heart's embrace,
Infinite wonders find their place.
Each thought a comet, bright and swift,
Channeling dreams, the greatest gift.

Through the cosmos, we navigate,
Embracing love, we elevate.
Sparks of hope in the darkest night,
Shimmering dreams take glorious flight.

Compassion's glow, a radiant sun,
Uniting the many, we bring as one.
In this vastness, we discover grace,
Galaxies thrive in each loving space.

Awakening the spirit's fire,
Energies rise, lifting higher.
As we embrace the worlds unseen,
We become the light that's ever keen.

The Cosmic Tapestry of Being

Threads of stardust, woven tight,
In the dark, we seek the light.
Every soul, a vibrant hue,
Painting the universe anew.

Time flows in an endless stream,
Every moment, a sacred dream.
Weaving tales of love and pain,
In the cosmic dance, we remain.

Elements bond in silent pact,
Connections formed, nothing lacks.
Universe vast, in unity we climb,
Every heartbeat sings like a chime.

The fabric shimmers, secrets weave,
In every thread, we dare believe.
Together we rise, together we fall,
A tapestry grand, embracing all.

With open hearts, we find our song,
In this vast cosmos, we belong.
The essence of life, an endless quest,
In every spirit, we are blessed.

Echoes from the Ether

Whispers dance on silent air,
Carried dreams from everywhere.
In shadows deep, the secrets flow,
A tapestry of tales we sow.

The stars ignite the endless night,
Guiding souls in silver light.
Each echo holds a hidden truth,
A song of ages, lost in youth.

Through timeless voids, their voices weave,
In every heart, they tug and cleave.
With every breath, the echoes swell,
A sacred story weaves its spell.

In the stillness, we feel their grace,
Filling every lonely space.
From whispered dreams to thunderous calls,
In every heartbeat, the silence falls.

Celestial Journeys of the Heart

In the cosmos, our spirits soar,
Through galaxies, forevermore.
Each step a dance, each glance a star,
We wander wild, no bounds, no bar.

With stardust trails, we write our fate,
In the quiet, we contemplate.
The universe, a canvas wide,
Where love and hope will always bide.

Across the moons, through twilight haze,
We seek the light of brighter days.
Our hearts entwined like cosmic rays,
Guiding us through life's endless maze.

Through every storm, our souls unite,
As constellations burn so bright.
Together we journey, hand in hand,
Across the sky, this timeless land.

Veiled in Celestial Light

Amidst the glow, our shadows play,
In whispers soft, we find our way.
The cosmos wraps us in its veil,
A hidden path, a secret trail.

With every star, a dream ignites,
We chase the dawn, we seek the nights.
In moonlit realms, our hearts entwine,
Veiled in light, our souls align.

Through cosmic winds, our spirits rise,
In galaxies where silence lies.
Each heartbeat echoes through the dark,
A spark of hope, a fleeting arc.

Veiled in dreams of endless skies,
We soar where timeless beauty lies.
In every breath, we find our song,
Together, where we both belong.

Echoing Through the Cosmos

In the void, our voices ring,
A cosmic chorus, we take wing.
With every note, the stars align,
An orchestra where dreams refine.

From distant shores, our echoes flow,
Through nebulae, the colors glow.
Each melody a fleeting spark,
Illuminating shadows dark.

With cosmic rhythms, hearts comply,
As constellations paint the sky.
We drift like whispers through the night,
Echoing love, igniting light.

In every silence, we find our sound,
Every longing, together bound.
Through endless space, our spirits roam,
Forever seeking, we find home.

Dance of the Etherial Spirits

In the hush of twilight's glow,
Whispers of dreams begin to flow.
Spirits twirl in a gentle sway,
Guided by the moon's soft play.

They weave through shadows, pure and bright,
Dancing under stars at night.
Each step, a note from the unseen,
Creating magic, serene, clean.

With laughter echoing in the air,
They spin without a single care.
In this realm where all is free,
Harmony hums in jubilee.

Their laughter blends with whispered songs,
Carried where the starlight throngs.
Ethereal glow, luminous thread,
Binding realms as dreams are fed.

As dawn approaches, shadows fade,
The spirits bow, their dance displayed.
Yet in the heart, their rhythms stay,
The dance persists in light of day.

Serenade of the Celestial Light

In silver beams that softly kiss,
The void transforms to boundless bliss.
Stars hum a tune that transcends time,
A serenade, celestial rhyme.

Galaxies swirl in graceful arcs,
Each note ignites cosmic sparks.
The universe hums a melo-dream,
Flowing like an endless stream.

Moonlight dances on the sea,
Whispering secrets, wild and free.
Notes drift on the breath of night,
Crafting beauty, pure delight.

Constellations join the choir,
Setting souls and hearts afire.
In harmony, the cosmos calls,
Its echoes fill celestial halls.

As stardust twinkles, dreams take flight,
Through realms of wonder, shining bright.
A serenade that knows no end,
In each heart, its love shall blend.

Lullabies from the Universe

Cradled in the cosmic sea,
Lullabies hum endlessly.
Stars entwined in night's embrace,
Whispering peace in boundless space.

Galactic sways and gentle tides,
In silence, starlit beauty hides.
The universe rocks the child of time,
In rhythms soft, pure and sublime.

Celestial echoes soothe the night,
Lulling hearts with radiant light.
Each note a soft and tender sigh,
Carried by the endless sky.

Nebulae sing their timeless song,
In harmony, where all belong.
Celestial tales, woven tight,
Embrace the darkness, bring forth light.

The universe whispers, "Rest, be still,"
With every twinkle, a gentle thrill.
In dreams, the cosmos holds you tight,
With lullabies from starry night.

Gazing into the Astral Abyss

Eyes wide open, stars unfold,
Glimmers of mysteries untold.
The astral abyss calls my name,
In its depths, a flickering flame.

Whispers of wisdom echo down,
Among the shadows, none will drown.
In silence deep, the cosmos speaks,
Revealing wonders to the meek.

Celestial visions dance and play,
Unveiling truths along the way.
As I gaze into the night,
I feel the universe's might.

Galactic realms invite my gaze,
Lost in spirals, I am amazed.
Through the void, I journey far,
Guided by the light of a star.

Each glimmer holds a tale of old,
In the silence, treasures unfold.
Gazing deep into the abyss,
I find the universe's kiss.

Stardust Whispers

In the night sky, secrets twirl,
Softly the stars begin to swirl.
Whispers of old, tales untold,
Magic unfolds in silver gold.

Glimmers dance on the cosmic sea,
A symphony sung by the galaxy.
Echoes of light in endless flight,
Infinite dreams ignite the night.

The moon casts shadows, gentle and wide,
Guiding lost souls on their ride.
Through the dark, they find their way,
In the warmth of dawn's soft ray.

Silent wishes take to the air,
Hearts ignited, we feel the flare.
Each stardust whisper, a fleeting glance,
A cosmic call, a celestial dance.

Hope is born under starlit skies,
In the universe, no goodbyes.
For in every sparkle, a story gleams,
Echoing softly, our shared dreams.

Luminous Echoes

Beneath the veil of evening's glow,
Luminous whispers begin to flow.
Stars collide in a fragrant night,
Sparks of existence, a breathtaking sight.

Faint melodies brush against the air,
Carried softly, a love laid bare.
In the cool grip of twilight's hand,
Hope unfurls like grains of sand.

As night deepens, time stands still,
Each echo a testament to free will.
Galaxies swirl in a cosmic dance,
Inviting hearts to dream and prance.

In the silence, we hear the throng,
Together in starry realms where we belong.
Every twinkle, a spark ignites,
Awakening passion in starlit nights.

Luminous echoes, sweet and divine,
Wrap us in warmth, the heavens entwine.
Across the universe, we find our place,
In the arms of light, a warm embrace.

Beneath the Galactic Veil

Under the vast, eternal embrace,
We wander through the cosmic space.
Stars shimmer like diamonds on high,
Silent guardians of the night sky.

Beneath the galactic veil we roam,
Finding in darkness, a joyful home.
Celestial wonders beckon our gaze,
Through the infinite, we drift and blaze.

In every twinkling, stories reside,
Galactic tales, where dreams abide.
Whispered secrets of distant lands,
Held in the universe's gentle hands.

Galaxies spin in a delicate waltz,
Inviting us deeper, with no faults.
Every moment, a kiss of time,
Suspended in silence, a perfect rhyme.

Stars weave a tapestry up above,
Crafting connections, all born of love.
Together we soar, in stardust we dwell,
Forever in awe, beneath the galactic veil.

Celestial Dreams Unfurled

In the cradle of night, dreams take flight,
Celestial visions dance with delight.
A canvas of stars, painted so bright,
Whispers of magic, igniting the night.

Flowing like rivers, stardust streams,
Sculpting the fabric of fragile dreams.
Each glimmer a promise, each spark a chance,
To know the universe in a timeless dance.

Among the planets, mysteries unfold,
Stories of courage and love retold.
With every heartbeat, we journey far,
Guided by the glow of a wandering star.

Lifting our souls to the heavens above,
Embracing the light and the warmth of love.
In the stillness, we hear the call,
Celestial dreams, uniting us all.

A horizon of hope as we reach for the sky,
With each gentle whisper, we're learning to fly.
Together we'll sail through the cosmic tide,
As we paint our stories on starlight's wide ride.

The Hidden Symphony of Stars

In the night's velvet embrace,
Stars weave tales of light,
Each whisper a gentle grace,
Echoes of the infinite bright.

From twilight's dark alluring cloak,
Harmony drifts on the breeze,
Notes of cosmic fables spoke,
Softly through the swaying trees.

Galaxies swirl in secret dance,
Music of the spheres unfold,
In this fleeting midnight trance,
Their stories long to be told.

Waves of starlight, a lullaby,
Lifting hearts beyond the night,
Within infinity's sigh,
We find our place in their flight.

Every spark a memory cast,
In the universe's gaze,
Together, we are unsurpassed,
In the harmony of stars we blaze.

Luminescence of the Soul's Odyssey

Through shadows of forgotten dawns,
The wandering spirit roams,
A journey where the light is drawn,
In search of celestial homes.

Awash in shimmering streams of fate,
The heart's echo leads the way,
Each step embraced by the innate,
Guiding towards a brighter day.

Whispers of the ancients call,
As luminescence paints the skies,
In the depths of night we stall,
To savor each moment that flies.

Each flicker a reminder sweet,
Of dreams that dare to intertwine,
In this odyssey we meet,
With the essence of the divine.

The light within begins to soar,
Illuminating paths we seek,
In the dance, we find much more,
A symphony in silence speaks.

In the Dance of Planetary Whispers

Around the sun, they twirl and spin,
Planets in a timeless waltz,
Each orbit a tale begins,
In harmony, find no faults.

Jupiter's might, a guardian bold,
While Venus shimmers with love,
In depths of night, stories unfold,
As the cosmos sings from above.

A dance of shadows, light plays coy,
Rings of Saturn shimmer in grace,
Echoes of joy, astral buoy,
As they trace a cosmic embrace.

Whispers in celestial tunes,
Gravitational hearts entwined,
In the cradle of stars and moons,
The universe shares what it finds.

Together they sway in endless time,
In the galaxy's tender hold,
A ballet of worlds, sublime,
With mysteries yet to behold.

Vibrations Across the Cosmic Tides

In the ocean of the dark expanse,
Galactic waves pulse and swell,
Ebbing rhythms form a trance,
As stardust weaves its spell.

Each vibration, a heart's soft thrum,
Resonating far and near,
In cosmic realms where dreams come,
The universe whispers clear.

Celestial harmonies collide,
In a fusion of light divine,
Where the essence of love resides,
And time and space intertwine.

Across the fabric, silent tides,
Every heartbeat, cosmic song,
With every pulse, the starlight guides,
Reminding us where we belong.

To dance upon these waves of night,
Is to know the endless grace,
In the cosmic tides of light,
We find our true embrace.

Ethereal Bonds of Time and Space

In the stillness of whispered dreams,
Ties weave through the fabric of night.
Echoes of laughter, distant beams,
Bringing our hearts to the light.

Gravity pulls with a gentle hand,
Carrying souls on a cosmic flight.
Together we rise, forever we stand,
In a dance of shadows and bright.

Moments collide in the vastness wide,
A tapestry rich with tales untold.
Across the galaxies, we reside,
Boundless wonders of stories unfold.

Eternally cradled in love so deep,
Stars chart the paths of our fate.
In the quiet, secrets softly seep,
An endless bond we create.

Time flows like rivers through our veins,
Weaving the past with the now.
In this journey, joy and pains,
Ethereal bonds, we avow.

Symphony of the Celestial Heart

A melody sings in the twilight air,
Notes drifting softly like petals of spring.
Harmony echoes, a love so rare,
In the silence, the cosmos does sing.

Stars compose in a grand ballet,
Each twinkle a note in the night sky.
In unison they dance, come what may,
A symphony played, we know not why.

Fill the void with your gentle grace,
Sound the alarms, let the worlds collide.
In this moment, we find our place,
With every heartbeat, love as our guide.

Whispers of planets, in rhythm they sway,
In perfect alignment, our dreams at last.
Together we forge, come what may,
A future bright, unbound by the past.

Feel the pulse of the universe rise,
As echoes of love surge and depart.
In this symphony, beneath starry skies,
We discover the beat of the celestial heart.

Shadows Beneath the Starlight

In the stillness, shadows grow,
Cascading whispers through the night.
Beneath the moon's soft, silvery glow,
Our secrets dance in fleeting light.

Echoes of stories linger near,
Stories of love, of grief, of grace.
In twilight's embrace, we shed our fear,
Finding solace in each other's space.

Stars twinkle like diamonds on high,
Painting dreams on the canvas vast.
In their shimmer, our hopes comply,
As shadows of yesterday fade fast.

Together we wander, hand in hand,
Through the dark, where mysteries lie.
With every heartbeat, we understand,
In shadows, our spirits learn to fly.

Beneath the starlight, hearts align,
In the dance of time, we traverse.
In the silence, love becomes divine,
A journey where shadows converse.

The Universe Within

In the depths of our very core,
Galaxies swirl in wondrous flight.
Infinite wonders we can't ignore,
The universe shines with pure light.

Each heartbeat tells a tale anew,
Every breath a promise unfurls.
Within us, the cosmos shines through,
Reflections of starlit pearls.

Awaken the spirits hidden deep,
Explore the realms of boundless skies.
In silence, our aspirations leap,
The universe beckons, arise.

Fleeting moments, like comets, grace,
Cradling dreams in soft, warm hands.
Together we soar, defying space,
Creating a world where love expands.

In the magic of inward exploration,
We find the stars that brightly gleam.
For within each soul lies creation,
The universe dances within our dream.

The Lure of Distant Horizons

Across the waves, the sun does chase,
A whisper soft, a gentle grace.
Where dreams ignite on the open sea,
The horizon calls, inviting me.

Each sail unfurls, a story told,
Of whispered winds and waters cold.
With every mile, I feel the pull,
To seek the vastness, to feel it full.

Amidst the clouds, the treasures lie,
In azure depths, where hopes can fly.
Adventure's breath in the salty air,
A distant land waits, beyond compare.

Chasing shadows, I wander far,
Guided only by the evening star.
The lure of freedom, wild and bold,
In every heartbeat, a tale unfolds.

With courage bright, I rise to roam,
Finding solace in the unknown home.
The journey matters, more than the end,
In skies of wonder, my spirit bends.

Origins Beneath Celestial Flames

Beneath the night, the stars ignite,
A tapestry of dreams, pure delight.
In cosmic dance, the spirits gleam,
We trace our roots, where stardust streams.

From ancient fires, we find our birth,
In whispered tales of the universe's worth.
Galaxies swirl in rhythmic embrace,
Illuminating histories time can't erase.

Each pulse, each flare, a story spun,
Of love and loss, of battles won.
We rise from ashes, forever reborn,
Embracing the light of the newly dawned.

The sky's vast canvas, our sacred tome,
Reflecting the journeys that lead us home.
In cosmic wonders, we seek our truth,
Under the gaze of eternal youth.

Now as I stand, beneath their glow,
I feel the power of ages flow.
We are the lords of this infinite night,
Bound by the stars, our spirits take flight.

Embracing the Infinite

In the stillness, where silence speaks,
I find the answers that my heart seeks.
The universe whispers, a gentle sigh,
Inviting my soul to eternally fly.

With open arms, I let it in,
Embracing the chaos, the world spins.
Every heartbeat is a boundless road,
Leading me forth, where dreams are sowed.

In the dance of existence, time unwinds,
Infinite moments, within us binds.
Through love and thought, we weave our fate,
An endless journey, to elevate.

As I drift among the galaxies bright,
Each spark becomes a guiding light.
With every breath, I weave the thread,
Of infinite stories, forever spread.

No boundaries hold, no fears remain,
In this vast expanse, I feel no pain.
I am the cosmos, boundless and free,
Embracing the infinite, I simply be.

Portraits of a Starborn Heart

In quiet moments, I glimpse the past,
Where echoes linger, shadows cast.
A heart born under the cosmic dome,
Painting colors that call me home.

Each heartbeat drums a tale of old,
Of love's embrace and stories bold.
Our spirit guides through space and time,
Creating rhythms, a sacred rhyme.

In starlit nights, my soul takes flight,
Carved in the fabric of endless night.
Each flicker tells of journeys wide,
Within this frame, my truth does bide.

Through the lens of dreams, I find my way,
A canvas painted in hues of gray.
Yet bursts of brilliance will break the dark,
Illuminating every loving spark.

With every pulse, my essence shines,
A portrait formed by sacred lines.
In the gallery of life, I play my part,
A soul eternal, a starborn heart.

Threads of Cosmic Harmony

In whispers soft, the cosmos sings,
Stars entwined in silken strings,
Galaxies dance in a velvet sea,
Echoes of love in infinity.

Planets spin in quiet grace,
Time and space in warm embrace,
Nebulas weave their vibrant threads,
As light cascades where silence treads.

Comets trace their fiery trails,
While distant suns weave fragrant tales,
Constellations map the ancient night,
Guiding souls to inner light.

Harmony flows through stardust veins,
Uniting hearts beyond the plains,
In every pulse, a rhythm grows,
A symphony that softly glows.

So let us stand beneath the skies,
And paint our dreams with cosmic eyes,
For in this dance, we all belong,
Threads of harmony, forever strong.

Night's Embrace of Dawn

In the twilight's tender glow,
Shadows blend in dance so slow,
Whispers of night begin to fade,
As dreams and light serenely wade.

Stars retreat with gentle sighs,
The moon dips low in velvet skies,
A hush settles on the earth,
As dawn awakens, heralding birth.

Crimson hues embrace the morn,
Nature stirs, a world reborn,
Birds sing sweet, a joyful tune,
As sunlight spills, chasing the moon.

In this moment, soft and rare,
Night's embrace whispers a prayer,
For in the balance, dark and bright,
Lies the beauty of day and night.

So let us cherish every hue,
In the dance of dark and dew,
For every dawn, like love, must rise,
In night's embrace, we find our skies.

Celestial Reveries

In starlit dreams, we drift away,
Where galaxies in silence play,
Each twinkling light a whispered thought,
In cosmic realms, where time is caught.

Nebulae bloom in colors bright,
Painting darkness with pure light,
We wander through this astral maze,
Lost in wonder, endless gaze.

The pulse of worlds beneath our feet,
Resonating with a cosmic beat,
We are but echoes in this dance,
Embracing fate, a timeless chance.

Celestial spirits guide our flight,
Through endless dreams of day and night,
In every sigh, a universe,
A realm where stars and hope converse.

So close your eyes and breathe it in,
Let celestial reveries begin,
For in the light of cosmic dreams,
We find our truth in stardust streams.

The Awakening of Celestial Echoes

From silence deep, the echoes rise,
Awakening in starry skies,
A gentle hum, a cosmic call,
Binding the fabric of us all.

Through galaxies, the whispers flow,
In perfect harmony, they glow,
As comets trace their age-old paths,
Revealing secrets in their swaths.

The turning worlds, a timeless dance,
In every heartbeat, there's a chance,
To hear the songs the heavens weave,
In the stillness, we believe.

Celestial voices sing of grace,
Uniting souls in endless space,
Awakening dreams long kept in sleep,
As stars light up the void so deep.

So listen close to the celestial sound,
For in their echoes, love is found,
In every note, a promise flows,
Awakening all that time bestows.

The Luminary Within

In the quiet depths of night,
A spark ignites, a soft glow bright.
Within our hearts, a flame does burn,
Guiding us all, our souls in turn.

Whispers of hope in shadows play,
Casting doubts and fears away.
Light emerges from the within,
A journey shared, where we begin.

Each thought a star, each dream a guide,
Through the darkness, we must reside.
With courage sewn into our seams,
We rise above, we dare to dream.

In every struggle, in each fight,
We cultivate our inner light.
Shimmering brightly, let it shine,
Together we stand, hearts intertwine.

The luminary glows so vast,
Embracing futures, letting go of past.
Together as one, we'll find our way,
In the warmth of love, we choose to stay.

Chasing the Light of Forgotten Stars

Upon the canvas of the sky,
Forgotten stars, they flicker high.
Chasing tales from ancient nights,
In every glimmer, hope ignites.

We wander lost, yet never stray,
In search of dreams that drift away.
With eyes aflame, we gaze above,
For what was once, we seek with love.

The echo of time whispers low,
Stories of the stars we know.
Each one a beacon, shining bright,
Guiding the hearts that yearn for light.

Through cosmic winds, we sail our fate,
Finding paths that resonate.
Emotions swirl like galaxies grand,
In the vastness of the stardust land.

We'll chase the light that guides our way,
Awakening dreams, come what may.
Together we'll dance on this cosmic stage,
Forever chasing, with hearts uncaged.

Emissaries of the Dark

In the shadows where secrets lay,
Something stirs, whispers stray.
Emissaries drawn from the night,
Bearing truths hidden from sight.

They wander with mysteries untold,
In their presence, we feel bold.
In darkness, they forge their fate,
Luminous souls that resonate.

Each step they take, a silent vow,
To unveil light in the here and now.
Guiding lost hearts through the haze,
With courage found in quiet ways.

From unseen realms, their wisdom flows,
In the midnight's embrace, it grows.
Transforming shadows into light,
Emissaries brightest in the night.

As night falls, we see their dance,
A cosmic waltz, a serendipitous chance.
Together we rise, before the dawn,
Embracing the dark, our fears are gone.

The Silent Language of Stars

In stillness of the night so deep,
Stars converse while the world sleeps.
A language soft, with luminescent grace,
Whispers of cosmos, an endless embrace.

Through twinkling eyes, they share their tales,
Of celestial journeys and cosmic trails.
Each point a story, waiting to be heard,
In the vast silence, not a single word.

With every glance, we seek to know,
The tales that travel from long ago.
In the silence, wisdom chimes,
Painting the night with ancient rhymes.

They speak of love, of dreams, of fate,
In the silent dance, our hearts relate.
With every heartbeat, we connect,
The language of stars, we are perfect.

So let us listen, let us learn,
From silent stars, their wisdom burns.
As we ponder, our spirits soar,
In the hush of night, we seek for more.

The Secret Life of Starlings

In murmurations they sway, a dance,
Fleeting shadows in twilight's glance.
Whispers of the wind they chase,
A secret world in the night they grace.

Beneath the fading hues of day,
Their flurry flickers, then slips away.
With each turn, a story unfolds,
In patterns of chaos, their lives told.

Through branches bare, they weave and dart,
Songs unspoken, a rhythm of heart.
Among the stars, they find their way,
In unity's strength, they choose to play.

From dusky skies to dusky ground,
In every pulse, a wisdom found.
The secret life, a marvelous show,
In each fleeting moment, their spirits glow.

When dawn breaks, their laughter flies,
A fading echo, a soft goodbye.
Yet in hearts, their memory sings,
In every soul, the joy it brings.

Astral Patterns in the Shadows

In the night where silence dwells,
Patterns rise from whispered spells.
Stars align in cosmic grace,
A dance of shadows, time and space.

Fleeting moments draw us near,
In astral visions, dreams appear.
Tracing pathways in the dark,
With every spark, a whispered arc.

Echoes linger, subtle, bright,
Guiding us through the velvet night.
Each constellation tells a tale,
Beneath the sky, we find the trail.

Steps are taken with soft intent,
In shadows' embrace, the mind is spent.
Patterns weave with every breath,
In the night's grandeur, we dance with death.

Through the unknown, we drift and glide,
In the stillness, we do not hide.
Astral whispers, our hearts in sync,
In cosmic flows, we pause to think.

Woven in Celestial Threads

In the fabric of the night, we find,
Threads of starlight intertwined.
Each silver strand, a tale to tell,
Woven dreams where shadows dwell.

Galaxies spin, a dance so grand,
In every flicker, a guiding hand.
Crafting stories in the void,
Celestial visions, never destroyed.

The tapestry unfolds with grace,
Patterns shifting, a cosmic embrace.
With every thread, a journey sown,
In the vastness, we are not alone.

Across the skies, our hopes ascend,
In starlit whispers, we descend.
Bound by dreams that softly spread,
In celestial threads, our souls are led.

With every heartbeat, the stars align,
In this moment, your light is mine.
Eternally woven, we take flight,
In the fabric of dreams, we ignite the night.

Thoughts Bathed in Galactic Light

In the stillness, thoughts arise,
Bathed in light from distant skies.
Galactic whispers, softly flow,
In every star, a spark to grow.

Moments flicker like a flame,
Illuminating thought's sweet game.
Each idea, a satellite's flight,
Journeying through the velvet night.

With wonder woven in our minds,
The universe in silence binds.
Through cosmic dances, we drift along,
In the embrace of the vast, we belong.

As daylight fades, reflections gleam,
Thoughts entwined in a lucid dream.
Bathed in glow, our spirits rise,
In the rhythm of the night, we realize.

In every heartbeat, galaxies sigh,
With each pulse, we learn to fly.
Thoughts bathed in light from above,
In the cosmos, we find our love.

Celestial Wings in a Sea of Night

In the stretch of velvet skies,
Stars awaken with soft sighs.
Moonlight dances on the sea,
Whispers of sweet ecstasy.

Beneath the shroud of endless dark,
Dreams ignite with a subtle spark.
Hearts aflame with cosmic glee,
Boundless joy, wild and free.

Galaxies swirl in graceful flight,
Painting shadows, pure delight.
Night's embrace, a sacred song,
Carrying souls where they belong.

In this realm of sighs and stars,
Rising high beyond the bars.
With wings that touch the void's expanse,
We soar, entranced in cosmic dance.

Here, in the silence of the vast,
Time suspends, forgetting past.
A million dreams, forever bright,
Celestial wings in a sea of night.

Beats of the Cosmic Heart

In the silence, pulses rise,
Rhythm flows through endless skies.
Galactic waves, a tender play,
Whispers of the Milky Way.

Each heartbeat, a star's embrace,
Echoing in the boundless space.
Time's fabric, woven tight,
Threads of day and threads of night.

Nebulas bright in hues divine,
Dancing to a sacred line.
In the cosmos, lost yet found,
Harmony in every sound.

Waves of light, shadows unfold,
Stories waiting to be told.
In the dark, a vibrant start,
Feel the beat of the cosmic heart.

As the universe spins and swirls,
Magic flows in graceful twirls.
Boundless love in spacetime's art,
Every pulse, a precious part.

A Journey Through Time's Veil

Step inside the swirling mist,
Moments lost, but not dismissed.
Each second weaves a tale anew,
Through time's veil, we wander through.

Echoes of the past arise,
In the light of fleeting skies.
Whispers linger, shadows play,
Guiding hearts along the way.

Paths untaken, dreams collide,
In the journey, we confide.
Memories like river streams,
Flowing softly toward our dreams.

Future beckons with open hands,
Drawing forth our wildest plans.
With every leap, we dare to find,
Threads of fate that life has twined.

Through the layers of the night,
We seek truth, we seek light.
Time's embrace, a soft, gentle sail,
In the journey through time's veil.

Beyond the Horizon of Existence

Where the earth meets the endless sky,
Dreamers gather, hearts held high.
Visions dance on the ocean's bend,
In the twilight, where dreams ascend.

Fading footsteps, yet we rise,
Chasing stars, transcending lies.
Voices whisper through the trees,
Echoing the cosmic breeze.

Beyond the waves, the secrets lie,
Holding truths that dare to fly.
In the depths of silence found,
Lies the essence, pure and sound.

Navigators of the soul's delight,
Charting paths in the soft twilight.
Each heartbeat is a distant call,
Drawing us beyond it all.

In this place where borders fade,
We find the dreams that time has made.
Beyond the horizon, we insist,
In realms of love, we coexist.

Secrets Within the Astral Paint

In colors deep, the cosmos speaks,
Whispers of stardust, truth it seeks.
Galaxies dance in silent night,
While secrets bloom in soft moonlight.

A canvas vast, where dreams unfold,
Brushstrokes of mysteries untold.
Every hue a tale once dreamed,
In the astral vast, lost hearts gleamed.

The planets sway in cosmic grace,
Echoes of laughter fill this place.
In every shade, the past persists,
As we wander through veils of mist.

Ancient chants in colors play,
Guiding seekers on their way.
The night reveals a hidden path,
In the silence, find its math.

So let us tread where starlights weave,
In cosmic art, we will believe.
For in each spark, a secret lies,
Within the paint, our spirit flies.

Celestial Waters of Memory

Ripples shimmer in twilight's glow,
Where time flows, soft and slow.
Each wave whispers a forgotten dream,
In celestial waters, we find our seam.

Mirrors of moments, lost in mist,
Every droplet tells what we've missed.
In depths profound, the memories sleep,
Guarding the past, their secrets keep.

We dive deep where the echoes play,
Through liquid stars, we drift away.
Searching for fragments of long-lost light,
In the embrace of the endless night.

The tides of fate pull us close,
As we navigate the cosmic dose.
In these waters, our hearts align,
We find solace in the divine.

So let the currents guide our way,
In celestial waves, we'll safely sway.
With each breath, we reclaim the past,
In these waters, memories last.

Navigating the Sea of Stars

Underneath the vast expanse,
We voyage with a hopeful glance.
Every star a beacon bright,
Guiding hearts through the night.

Waves of light crash on our skin,
As we journey where dreams begin.
The constellations map our course,
Fueling our souls with unseen force.

With every breath, the cosmos calls,
Echoing softly as starlight falls.
In this ocean, we sail free,
Navigating our destiny.

The winds of time carry us far,
With hopes as bright as the evening star.
Through nebulae's glow, we find our way,
In the sea of stars, we choose to stay.

So let the universe lift our sails,
With cosmic currents, we will prevail.
As navigators of the ethereal sea,
Together we'll chart our own journey.

The Cradle of Cosmic Wonder

In starlit arms, the universe dreams,
Where light cascades in silver beams.
This cradle holds the night so tight,
Fostering hope, igniting light.

Each twinkle tells a story grand,
Woven in time by nature's hand.
In silence, mysteries start to stir,
Whispering tales to those who purr.

As galaxies spin in gentle grace,
We find ourselves in their embrace.
The wonder of life, a fleeting glance,
In cosmic rhythms, we take a chance.

Through nebulous mists, our spirits soar,
Awakening the hearts that seek for more.
In the cradle, magic takes flight,
Transforming shadows into light.

So let us marvel at the night's sweet song,
In this cradle, we all belong.
For in the wonders of the celestial sea,
We find our truth and set it free.

The Glow Beneath My Skin

In shadows deep, a light does weave,
A whisper soft, that I believe.
It dances there in every vein,
A pulse of warmth, joy and pain.

It flickers bright when moments call,
A beacon wild, it won't let fall.
The urge for life, for love so pure,
In this bright glow, I feel secure.

Though storms may come and skies turn gray,
The fire inside will find its way.
Transforming fears to strength within,
This is the glow beneath my skin.

Each heartbeat sings, a soft refrain,
A melody from joy and pain.
With every breath, it comes alive,
A sacred light that helps me thrive.

So let it shine, this force divine,
A guiding star, forever mine.
In darkest nights, the light will burst,
Awakening the deepest thirst.

Harmonies of the Night Sky

Beneath the stars, a song unfolds,
In whispered notes, the night beholds.
Each twinkling light, a voice so clear,
Together singing, far and near.

The moonlight spills like silver threads,
Weaving dreams in peaceful beds.
A symphony of gentle sighs,
Nature's breath, beneath dark skies.

In quiet nights, the world is still,
The heart finds space, a perfect fill.
With every pulse, the cosmos sways,
To harmonies the spirit plays.

The constellations softly glide,
With whispered secrets tucked inside.
A dance of shadows, light takes flight,
In the embrace of endless night.

So listen close and feel the tune,
The melody of stars and moon.
In every note, a world to find,
The harmonies that bind mankind.

Chronicles of the Infinite

In endless realms where stories dwell,
A tapestry of hope to tell.
Each thread a life, a moment spun,
Chronicles of all, we have begun.

Time flows like rivers, vast and wide,
Echoes of paths where dreams reside.
In every choice, a branch unfolds,
Infinite tales, waiting to be told.

With every sunrise, a page turns bright,
Casting shadows, embracing light.
The past and future meet today,
In this grand tome, we find our way.

Whispers of wisdom in the air,
Nature speaks, if we will care.
To learn from ages gone before,
Is to unlock the hidden door.

So pen your story, let it flow,
In this vast book, let your heart glow.
For in each life, we find the spark,
The chronicles of the infinite arc.

A Symphony of Starlight

A canvas stretched across the night,
With brushstrokes bold, of purest light.
Each star a note, a cosmic sound,
In harmony, our hearts are bound.

The universe sings in colors bright,
In every hue, a spark of light.
With melodies that twist and weave,
The fabric of the dreams we believe.

As whispers of the cosmos play,
Guiding us through night and day.
In every glance, a story clear,
The symphony we hold so dear.

So close your eyes and feel the beat,
In starlit skies, our souls can meet.
With every rhythm, vast and free,
A symphony of you and me.

In this grand dance, we find our place,
Within the stars, the timeless grace.
With every heartbeat, we arise,
To join the song across the skies.

In the Shadow of the Moon

Silken shadows dance and sway,
Underneath the moon's soft ray.
Whispers linger in the night,
As dreams take flight out of sight.

Stars like diamonds blink above,
Calling forth the world's sweet love.
Each heartbeat echoes in the dark,
Igniting every hidden spark.

The silver beams caress the ground,
In silence, magic can be found.
Mysteries wrapped in lunar light,
Guide the way through endless night.

Pulse of the Celestial Veil

Beneath the vast celestial dome,
The universe feels just like home.
Stars pulse with a vibrant glow,
Their ancient tales begin to flow.

In constellations, secrets lie,
Whispered softly to the sky.
Galaxies spin in graceful dance,
Inviting all to take a chance.

Embrace the rhythm, feel the beat,
In the cosmos, our hearts meet.
Every pulse, a heartbeat shared,
In this beauty, we are spared.

Celestial Orbs in a Harmonious Flight

Planets twirl with timeless grace,
Each one finds its perfect place.
In the vastness, they unite,
Chasing dreams within the night.

Moons and stars in a dance divine,
Weaving through the space and time.
Their song travels far and wide,
Through the cosmos, like the tide.

Harmony in every spin,
A cosmic tale that dwells within.
Each orb glows with a vibrant spark,
Illuminating paths in the dark.

The Canvas of Oblivion and Emergence

In the void, colors intertwine,
A canvas drawn, both bold and fine.
Oblivion swirls with fiery glow,
From chaos, new wonders grow.

Each brushstroke weaves a new tale,
Emergence rises, never frail.
From shadows deep, light finds a way,
Awakening life within the gray.

The universe sings in vibrant hues,
A dance of fate, a choice of views.
In every corner, creation breathes,
Through the silence, beauty weaves.

Underneath a Canopy of Stars

Beneath the sky, where whispers play,
The stars illuminate the night's ballet.
Dreams take flight in velvet hue,
As constellations tell tales anew.

Gentle breezes caress the leaves,
Nature whispers secrets, weaving weaves.
In this magic, hearts align,
As we find solace, pure and divine.

The moon hangs low, a silver crest,
While shadows dance in quiet jest.
Every twinkle holds a mystery,
Inviting us to share the history.

Night blooms softly like a flower,
Each moment cherished, enchanted hour.
To journey on this astral sea,
Is to embrace pure harmony.

Whispers of secrets float on the air,
Underneath the stars, beyond compare.
Together we roam in this night's embrace,
In the cosmos' arms, we find our place.

Celestial Pathways and Moonlit Ways

In the hush of night, we wander free,
Celestial pathways beckon to me.
Moonlit ways guide our gentle tread,
Where dreams unfurl and spirits are fed.

Stardust trails kiss the earth below,
As we follow the light's tender glow.
Through cosmic dances, we weave and sway,
In the softness of night, come what may.

The symphony of silence sings,
Eternal magic the nighttime brings.
With every step, we glimpse the divine,
As moonbeams form a radiant line.

Stars above like diamonds bright,
Illuminate thoughts hidden from sight.
In this moment, we hold time still,
In celestial rhythms, our hearts will fill.

Together, we soar through space and dream,
In harmony where colors gleam.
Guided by starlight in endless maze,
We lose ourselves in these moonlit ways.

The Language of Light

In shimmering threads, the cosmos speaks,
The language of light, with wisdom it leaks.
Painting the night with colors so bright,
Each hue a story, a whispered delight.

Sparks of the stars dance across the sky,
Telling of wonders that never die.
Fleeting moments in twilight's embrace,
A timeless ballet through vastness of space.

Under the spell of the luminous glow,
Conversations with shadows, soft and slow.
Eyes locked in wonder, hearts intertwined,
In the warmth of the light, true love we find.

The sun's golden rays bring warmth to our skin,
In daylight's embrace, our journey begins.
With every sunrise, new dreams take flight,
In the glorious dawn, we bask in light.

Let the brilliance guide us, hand in hand,
Navigating realms both simple and grand.
For in the tapestry of day and night,
We learn the true meaning of the light.

Embracing Astral Whispers

In the stillness, whispers arise,
Echoes of dreams beneath open skies.
Stars engage in a tender dance,
Inviting us into their timeless trance.

Every sigh of the night winds low,
Carries secrets that only stars know.
The cosmos speaks in gentle tones,
Revealing truths in celestial moans.

In shadows deep, where silence hums,
A symphony of galaxies comes.
As constellations weave tales of old,
Our hearts are sparked, enchanted and bold.

Under the watch of the moon's soft gaze,
We lose ourselves in the night's sweet praise.
Each twinkle a promise of journeys ahead,
Guiding our steps as we forge and tread.

Embracing the whispers, we find our way,
Through the vastness of night and the break of day.
With every heartbeat, our spirits unite,
In the embrace of the magic, pure and bright.

Stardust Serenades

In the quiet night sky, stars gleam,
Whispers of dreams, so gentle, they seem.
Floating on breezes, soft and bright,
Embracing the darkness, bringing in light.

Galaxies twirl in cosmic embrace,
Melodies echo through time and space.
Each twinkle a tale, a lost lullaby,
Sung by the heavens, where wishes fly.

Threads of silver weave through the dark,
Lighting the path with a radiant spark.
Together they dance, in celestial grace,
Guiding the wanderers from place to place.

A symphony rises, pure and profound,
As stardust gathers, love's notes abound.
Hearts beat in rhythm with beats of the night,
Finding their way in the glow of starlight.

In this serenade, let spirits unite,
Echoes of joy in the soft velvet light.
Together we soar through infinite skies,
A chorus of wonder, where true magic lies.

The Harmony of Astral Beats

Beneath the celestial rhythm, we sway,
In the silence of night, we drift and play.
Stars pulse in time, a mystical song,
Carried on whispers, where we all belong.

Infinity shimmers with each gentle beat,
Drawing us closer, as hearts skip a beat.
In the dance of the cosmos, we find our way,
Melodies guiding our dreams, night and day.

Orbs of light flicker, a radiant glow,
Pulsing like hearts in the depths below.
Cosmic winds carry our secrets so deep,
In the harmony of night, we wake from sleep.

Echoes of love resonate through the stars,
Connecting the dots of our lives and scars.
With every heartbeat, a story unfolds,
In the tapestry woven with threads of gold.

Let us dance in the silence, hearts intertwined,
With each astral beat, possibilities aligned.
In the night's embrace, we rise and ascend,
To the rhythm of cosmos, where journeys blend.

Threads of Light and Darkness

In shadows we tread, where light softly glows,
Through whispers of starlight, the universe flows.
Balancing spirals of dark and of bright,
We weave our existence in day and in night.

Each moment a thread, fragile yet strong,
Binding the echoes of right and of wrong.
In the tapestry woven with care from our birth,
We find our stories, our joys and our mirth.

The darkness holds secrets, the light brings release,
Together they dance, a circle of peace.
In the embrace of the quiet, we find our way,
Learning to cherish both night and the day.

With every heartbeat, the threads intertwine,
Creating a fabric both subtle and fine.
In the delicate balance of shadows and beams,
We find our strength in the depths of our dreams.

So let us explore the vastness and depth,
For in every shadow, new light's adept.
Together we journey, diverse paths we trace,
In threads of light and darkness, we find our place.

A Dance Among the Stars

Stars sparkle brightly, a cosmic ballet,
Whirling and twirling, a grand cabaret.
Galaxies shimmer, in rhythmic embrace,
Inviting all dreamers to join in the race.

Together we spin under skies so wide,
With each step a journey, with love as our guide.
As the universe sways to a timeless beat,
We lose ourselves in the magic we meet.

The night is alive with the song of the spheres,
Echoing dreams through the passage of years.
Hands raised to heavens in pure jubilation,
Embracing the wonder, lost in elation.

With the pulse of the cosmos beneath our feet,
We dance to the rhythm, a moment so sweet.
Under the gaze of the moon's gentle gleam,
We twirl and we twist, caught up in a dream.

In this dance among stars, let hearts intertwine,
Bound by the wonders, the sacred divine.
As we sway with the night, through the vastness we roam,

In a celestial embrace, we find our true home.

The Heart of Cosmic Stillness

In twilight's hush, the stars align,
Whispers of peace in the night's design.
A breath of space, an ageless grace,
In cosmic stillness, we find our place.

Galaxies dance in silent embrace,
Time drifts softly, a gentle trace.
Each heartbeat echoes, calm and clear,
In the vast expanse, we lose our fear.

Crickets hum their night-time song,
In stillness, where we all belong.
The universe breathes, a tender friend,
In quiet moments, our souls transcend.

Eternal whispers in the void,
Moments of peace, anxiety destroyed.
We linger in shadows, light takes its form,
In cosmic stillness, our hearts grow warm.

Nestled beneath the celestial dome,
In the heart of stillness, we find our home.
Time stands still in this sacred space,
The heart of cosmic stillness, a warm embrace.

Nebulae of the Mind

In the depths of thoughts, colors bloom,
Nebulae swirling, dispelling gloom.
Imagination's dance paints the night,
In the canvas of dreams, we find our light.

Ideas collide like stars in flight,
Crafting new worlds in the dark of night.
Each spark a whisper, a tale untold,
In the mind's vast cosmos, wonders unfold.

Past and future, a swirling tide,
In nebulae of thought, we glide.
Fragments of time in radiant hues,
Crafting our paths, discovering truths.

Riddles of starlight, mysteries deep,
In the nebula, knowledge we keep.
Connections forged in the ether's embrace,
In the realm of the mind, we find our place.

Thoughts intertwine, like constellations bright,
Awakening dreams, igniting the night.
In the galaxy of self, we redefine,
Exploring the vastness, nebulae of the mind.

Ethereal Resonance

In softest tones, the spirit sings,
Ethereal echoes, gentle wings.
In the twilight hush, harmonies play,
Resonance lingers in the end of day.

Vibrations dance like whispers of breeze,
In the silence, hearts find their ease.
Each note a heartbeat, a pulse divine,
In ethereal waves, we intertwine.

Chords of the cosmos, melodies mild,
In unity's grasp, we are beguiled.
Moments expand, infinity's song,
In the web of existence, we belong.

Across the spectrum of time we float,
In resonance, every soul is a note.
We tune to the heartbeat of all that is free,
Ethereal whispers lead us to be.

In stillness we wander, our spirits aligned,
In this sacred space, pure love defined.
With every heartbeat, and every breath,
In ethereal resonance, we conquer death.

Moonlit Contemplations

Beneath the moon's soft, silver glow,
Silent thoughts like rivers flow.
In the quiet night, secrets unfurl,
Whispers of dreams in a slumbering world.

Stars shimmer gently in the sky's embrace,
Guiding our hearts to a tranquil place.
Each beam a promise of hope and light,
In moonlit contemplations, we take flight.

Reflections dance on the water's face,
In deep stillness, we find our space.
The universe listens as we ponder and sigh,
With every question, new answers arise.

In shadows of silver, our fears unwind,
With every heartbeat, new truths we find.
The night holds wisdom, ancient and wise,
In moonlit contemplations, our spirits rise.

As dawn's first light begins to break,
With grateful hearts, new paths we take.
Under the moon's watchful gaze, we weave,
In contemplative stillness, we truly believe.

Whispers of Starlit Dreams

In the still of night's embrace,
Soft whispers dance through space.
Stars twinkle with secrets old,
In their glow, our hearts unfold.

Dreams float like clouds on high,
Beneath the vast and endless sky.
We chase the echoes of the light,
Guided by the moon so bright.

Silent wishes take their flight,
Carried forth by cosmic light.
Through the darkness, hope will gleam,
Lost in whispers of a dream.

Night's canvas painted deep,
Where starlight and silence seep.
Every twinkle, a story told,
The universe's magic unfolds.

With every glimmer, we align,
In the shadows, our hearts entwine.
For in each pulse of bright desires,
Live the whispers of our fires.

Echoes of the Infinite Sky

In the vastness, a soft sigh,
Echoes dance in the infinite sky.
Clouds drift like thoughts in flight,
Carrying dreams into the night.

Stars shimmer with ancient tales,
Woven in the cosmic gales.
Their light calls to hearts so free,
Echoing through eternity.

Moments linger, pause in time,
With each pulse, a silent rhyme.
Galaxies spin, stories collide,
In the dark, we seek to glide.

Every twinkle, a gentle nudge,
Where wonder and time won't budge.
Floating softly on a breeze,
Part of all that's meant to tease.

With every breath, the night reveals,
Secrets that the stillness seals.
In the echoes of the vast orbs,
We find solace, our spirit absorbs.

Chasing Moonlit Shadows

Beneath the gaze of the silver moon,
Shadows flicker, a whispered tune.
We wander paths of softest glow,
In the night, our dreams will flow.

The world asleep, our hearts awake,
In every sigh, a chance we take.
Moonlight weaves with gentle grace,
Leading us to a secret place.

Rippling waters charm the night,
Mirroring stars, a breathtaking sight.
With each step, the shadows play,
Guiding us in a mystic ballet.

Hand in hand, we roam together,
Underneath the soft, warm weather.
The shadows dance, a fleeting thrill,
Chasing whispers until we are still.

In the calm, our souls ignite,
Chasing dreams in the stolen light.
For in the quiet, hearts collide,
As we chase shadows, side by side.

The Heartbeat of Cosmic Waves

In the rhythm of the endless night,
Cosmic waves pulse with pure delight.
Each heartbeat echoes through the void,
In this dance, we are deployed.

Stars hum softly, a tranquil song,
Leading our spirits where they belong.
Across the canvas of the dark,
We find the light, the hidden spark.

Galaxies swirl, a vibrant stream,
Alive with color, hearts dream.
The universe breathes with every sigh,
In its embrace, we soar high.

Time dissolves like morning mist,
In this moment, nothing is amiss.
The heartbeat carries, vast and free,
A cosmic bond, you and me.

So let us ride the waves of grace,
In the heartbeat of this boundless space.
Together we dance, forever we play,
In the rhythms of cosmic waves, we stay.

The Universe Within

In silence deep, a spark ignites,
The whispers of the hidden sights.
In shadows dance the thoughts untold,
A galaxy of dreams unfolds.

The heart's expanse, a cosmos wide,
Where secrets of the soul abide.
Like stars that twinkle in the night,
Each thought a beacon, pure and bright.

Within our minds, a world we make,
A tapestry of joy and ache.
With every heartbeat, worlds collide,
A universe we cannot hide.

Through storms of doubt, we seek the light,
In depths of fear, we rise in flight.
For in our core, all life begins,
The universe within us spins.

So journey forth, explore the vast,
In every moment, hold it fast.
With open heart, embrace the sound,
The universe within is found.

Silent Songs of the Skies

Beneath the quilt of velvet night,
The stars ignite, a pure delight.
In whispered winds, the moonlight beams,
A symphony born of our dreams.

The clouds, like ships, sail high and free,
Carrying secrets over the sea.
Each breeze a note, soft and profound,
In silent songs that know no sound.

As daylight fades, the colors blend,
In twilight's grasp, the echoes mend.
The softest hum, a gentle grace,
In nature's choir, we find our place.

With every sigh, the stars reply,
A timeless dance, the earth and sky.
In stillness found, our spirits rise,
To the silent songs of the skies.

So listen close, let your heart soar,
For in the silence, there's so much more.
With open eyes, embrace the night,
In silent songs, we find the light.

Cosmic Journeys in Solitude

In solitary whispers, we roam,
Through galaxies, we find our home.
The stars our guides, so far yet near,
In cosmic journeys, we shed fear.

The path unfolds in quiet grace,
Each step a dance, a sacred space.
With every breath, the universe sighs,
A lonely heart learns how to rise.

Through nebulae of thoughts we glide,
On waves of silence, hearts collide.
In solitude, the light is found,
A cosmic song, an endless sound.

So take the leap, embrace the vast,
In stillness search, release the past.
For in your soul, the stars align,
Cosmic journeys, truly divine.

In every moment, grace appears,
In solitude, dissolve your fears.
With open arms, the truth will show,
The path of light where we must go.

Illuminated Paths of the Soul

Through shadows deep, we seek the flame,
Each step we take, a dance, a claim.
In light we find the way to heal,
Illuminated paths reveal.

With every dawn, the colors spread,
Painting dreams in gold and red.
The echoes of our hearts resound,
A sacred journey, joy unbound.

With every breath, we weave the light,
A tapestry of day and night.
The path before us, bright and bold,
In every story, love is told.

So take my hand, we'll forge ahead,
In fields of light, where hope is bred.
With every heartbeat, let it flow,
Illuminated paths we'll know.

In trust we walk, with spirits high,
Through valleys low and mountains nigh.
For in the heart, the truth unfolds,
Illuminated paths of souls.

Transcendence in the Nightscape

In shadows deep the stars do gleam,
Whispers of night, a silent dream.
Softly they weave through the void so vast,
Echoing tales of ages past.

Moonlight dances on silver streams,
Illuminating the heart that beams.
Each twinkle calls a soul to soar,
Beyond the realms of evermore.

The breeze carries secrets untold,
Of journeys woven in starlit gold.
A lullaby sweet, serene and bold,
Wrapped in the night, a quest unfolds.

Footsteps echo on pathways bright,
Guided by dreams in the shroud of night.
Transcendental visions beckon near,
Inviting each wanderer without fear.

As dusk bids farewell to the day,
Celestial wonders come out to play.
Lost in the depths of the night so grand,
With each heartbeat, the cosmos expands.

Portals of Luminescent Dreams

In verdant fields where shadows sway,
The flicker of fireflies leads the way.
Portals open in the night so bright,
Inviting all to a realm of light.

Whispers of magic dance in the air,
As dreams awaken, free without care.
Colors blend in a vibrant stream,
Painting the canvas of hope and dream.

Each step unfolds a path unknown,
Where moments fleeting are gently sown.
A bridge between worlds, silent yet clear,
Drawing all hearts to the wonders near.

Glow of the stars in their shimmering dress,
Guide the lost souls through cosmic finesse.
With every heartbeat, a pulse of gleam,
Life intertwined with the fabric of dream.

Through the night, in a dance with fate,
The portals beckon, seduce, create.
A journey embarked with every sigh,
In luminescence, our spirits fly.

The Essence of Infinite Space

In the cradle of night, the cosmos lays,
Infinity whispers in mystical ways.
Stars like jewels in a velvet sea,
Each pulse of light, a reverie.

A tapestry woven from dreams unspoken,
Each thread a truth, a heart unbroken.
Time unfurls in a silent embrace,
Holding the essence of infinite space.

Galaxies swirl in a grand ballet,
Cosmic rhythms in celestial sway.
The universe hums, a harmonious song,
Echoing chants of where we belong.

In the silence, mysteries await,
Waiting to unveil the soul's true state.
A dance of light and shadow entwined,
In the depths of space, our spirits aligned.

Eternity beckons with open hands,
Inviting us to wander through distant lands.
In every heartbeat, we find our place,
Within the essence of infinite space.

Illuminating the Cosmic Trail

Across the vastness where stardust dwells,
Many stories in silence tell.
The cosmic trail with its radiant glow,
Guiding us onward wherever we go.

Nebulas bloom in colors bright,
Painting the darkness with brilliant light.
Each lightyear traveled, a moment's grace,
Connecting all through the boundless space.

Whirls of galaxies, a cosmic dance,
Life taking shape in a fateful chance.
With every step, we illuminate,
A journey shared we contemplate.

Constellations sketch the stories we seek,
In the universe's arms, we are unique.
Illuminating paths where wonders prevail,
Guided by dreams along the cosmic trail.

When the world slows and whispers cease,
We find our purpose, our sense of peace.
With hearts wide open, we embrace the night,
Illuminating our souls with starlit light.

.

www.ingramcontent.com/pod-product-compliance
Ingram Content Group UK Ltd.
Pitfield, Milton Keynes, MK11 3LW, UK
UKHW021530210125
4208UKWH00025B/544

9 781805 618539